Fergana

Osh

Kashgar

Dunghuang

hawar

The Himalayas

Xi'an

R. Sutlej

Panipat

Delhi

Agra

R.Yamuna

Gwalior

R.Ganges

Bay Of Bengal

THE STORY OF
Babur

PARVATI SHARMA

ILLUSTRATIONS by URMIMALA NAG

Good earth
A Goodearth Publication

PUFFIN BOOKS

A GOODEARTH PUBLICATION
Eicher Goodearth Private Limited
Registered Office: 3rd Floor, Select Citywalk, A-3, District Centre, Saket, New Delhi - 110017
www.goodearth.in

In collaboration with

PUFFIN BOOKS
Published by the Penguin Group
Penguin Books India Pvt. Ltd, 7th Floor, Infinity Tower C, DLF Cyber City, Gurgaon 122 002, Haryana, India
Penguin Group (USA) Inc., 375 Hudson Street, New York, New York 10014, USA
Penguin Group (Canada), 90 Eglinton Avenue East, Suite 700, Toronto, Ontario, M4P 2Y3, Canada
Penguin Books Ltd, 80 Strand, London WC2R 0RL, England
Penguin Ireland, 25 St Stephen's Green, Dublin 2, Ireland (a division of Penguin Books Ltd)
Penguin Group (Australia), 707 Collins Street, Melbourne, Victoria 3008, Australia
Penguin Group (NZ), 67 Apollo Drive, Rosedale, Auckland 0632, New Zealand
Penguin Books (South Africa) (Pty) Ltd, Block D, Rosebank Office Park, 181 Jan Smuts Avenue, Parktown North,
Johannesburg 2193, South Africa

Penguin Books Ltd, Registered Offices: 80 Strand, London WC2R 0RL, England

First published by Eicher Goodearth Private Limited and Penguin Books India 2015

Copyright © Eicher Goodearth Private Limited 2015
Text by Parvati Sharma
Illustrations copyright © Urmimala Nag 2015
Design and Layout : Arya Nerker, Manish Aggarwal

ISBN 9780143334132

Typeset in DellaRobbia BT
Printed at Thomson Press India Ltd, New Delhi

A NOTE ON THE BOOK

This book is based largely on Babur's autobiography, the Babur Nama. For the most part, events and characters appear as Babur described them. However, for the sake of brevity and continuity, many details of his life have been left out, some conflated, while others have been invented.

For example, Babur conquered (and lost) Samarkand three times. Here, these upheavals are condensed into one. Again, though we know that someone brought gunpowder to Babur, we don't know who, because those parts of the Babur Nama are missing. However, we do know that Ustad Ali-Quli was Babur's Master of Guns. The story of Babur's death is a legend.

For anyone who wants to read more of Babur in his own words, *The Baburnama: Memoirs of Babur, Prince and Emperor* translated by Wheeler M. Thackston (The Modern Library, 2002) is highly recommended.

A PENGUIN RANDOM HOUSE COMPANY

Contents

THE BEGINNING

A long time ago, before you were born, or your mother was born, or your father was born, or your grandparents were born, or even your *grandparents' grandparents* were born, there was a king called Umar Shaikh. Umar Shaikh ruled Fergana, and to reach Fergana, you had to swim across cold, blue rivers, and you had to climb up tall, white mountains, and you had to ride your horse for many long days — because Fergana was really far away.

But once you got there, you'd be very happy, because Fergana was a lovely and beautiful place, full of green fields to run in, and ponds to swim in, and trees to climb. And it was particularly full of delicious things to eat.

The pears of Fergana were called nashpati, and these nashpatis were so big that when you bit one, all the sugary syrup would flow down your chin and into your

collar, as if you were drinking juice.
Pomegranates were called anaar,
and their seeds were
like big red marbles.
Everyone agreed
mirtimuri melons
were the best in
the world, and even
the almonds were
crunchy like sweets. Fat
pheasants waddled about under the
fruit trees, and you could reach out
and pick one up for your dinner
as you walked along.

Everyone in Fergana liked to eat, and King Umar Shaikh liked to eat most of all. On special occasions, like birthdays, Umar Shaikh would throw a party for all Fergana, a feast in which everyone would eat desserts and drink sherbets and play polo and swim all day. After the feast, Umar Shaikh would stand up, and all the guests would hold their breaths, and everyone would stop talking . . . and wait.

You see, at the end of every feast in Fergana, Umar Shaikh would stand and stretch his hands in the air, and he would take a deep breath and he would say a big YUM — and then, one by one, the buttons of his jacket would begin to go . . .

POP!

POP–a–POP!

POP–a–POP–a–POP! *POP!*

like fire-crackers. And only after this had happened did everyone go home.

Now Umar Shaikh had a son called Zahiruddin. When Zahiruddin was very small, he liked to crawl on his hands and knees, pretending to be a tiger. "Rowr!" he would say to his father, when Umar Shaikh was sitting on his throne. "Rowr!" he would say to Aaneh, his mother, when she was combing her hair in the bedroom.

"Rowr, rowr!" he would say to Nene, his grandmother, when she was writing a book under a tree in the palace garden. And everyone would jump up in fright and cry, "A tiger has come to eat me!" — and Zahiruddin would be very pleased with himself.

Finally, one day, Nene went to Umar Shaikh and said, "Don't you think Zahiruddin is too big a name for such a small boy? I think we should call him Little Tiger instead, because that is what he seems to be, in his soul." Umar Shaikh agreed, and from then on, everyone called his son Babur. And when his Rowrs! were really loud, they called him Baboor.

That, you see, is what they call little tigers in Fergana.

A SPARKLY CITY

For Babur's fifth birthday, his family took him to Samarkand, which was a kingdom far away to the west. It was so far away, in fact, that you needed a week to get there, so everyone was quite tired when they reached. Nene, in her carriage, had fallen asleep. Umar Shaikh, on his horse, was drooping like a thirsty rose. And Babur, riding his favourite pony, was getting quite bored and not a little cranky.

But then, the Iron Gate of Samarkand rolled open before them, and suddenly nobody was tired any more. Nene sat up with a start and smiled. Umar Shaikh straightened his back and adjusted his turban. And Babur? Well Babur looked all around him, this way and that way, and his eyes grew big as apricots and his mouth fell open all on its own and it said a simple, single "Wah!"

The thing is, you see, Fergana was a valley. A valley has green hills
and cold springs and sweet fruit trees, and makes a lovely kingdom.
But there is one thing it isn't and cannot be, and that is: a city.

Samarkand, now, *that* was a city. It had buildings that rose to the sky,
and its streets were never-ending and full of countless people, all doing
countless things. Babur craned his neck, trying to see what they were up
to. One man was selling hot, soft bread that filled the air with the smell
of sugar and raisins. A fat woman in a blue cape was juggling wooden
balls. A tall man in red trousers was plucking at the
strings of his rubab.

There were so many people, and the streets
were so full of chatter and buzz, and the buildings
were painted in such shining colours, that Babur
began to feel quite dizzy and he thought he
might fall off his pony. Luckily, just then,
they reached the palace.

There are many ways to describe a palace. You can say it is bigger than ten houses. Or you can say it is taller than ten trees. But there was only one way to describe the Palace of Samarkand. It was sparkly, like a star.

"Wah!" said Babur. But he said it in a small whisper, because the sparkliness was making him a little scared.

Umar Shaikh took Babur's small hand in his and said,

"Do you like it, Little Tiger?

This is the palace of your great-great-*great*-grandfather Temur, the bravest soldier and richest king the world has ever known. Your uncle Sultan Ahmad Mirza lives here now, and he rules Samarkand the way I rule Fergana. Go now, run and find him, and maybe he will give us some lunch. Because I, for one, am very hungry." And Umar Shaikh patted his round stomach in a way that made Babur less afraid.

Babur, his parents and his Nene spent one month in Samarkand.

The grown-ups liked to go to the forest and hunt, and they liked to go to the market and shop for things like paper and velvet, and they really liked to talk and talk for hours after dinner. Babur played with his sister Khanzada and Sultan Ahmad Mirza's daughter, who was called Ayesha.

On the day they were leaving, everyone gathered at the Iron Gate and Umar Shaikh asked his son, "Well, Babur, did you have a nice time in Samarkand?"

"Yes," said Babur, "I like it very much here. Will we come back soon?"

"Of course. And when you are older, would you like to come back and marry Ayesha?"

"Oh no, thank you" said Babur, politely. "I would prefer to come back and be King of Samarkand."

Umar Shaikh laughed so loudly at this that he POPPED quite a few buttons. Sultan Ahmad Mirza laughed too, but not so much. And they both patted each others' backs and ruffled Babur's hair the way grown-ups like to do, and said, "Well, well. Who knows what the future will bring?"

MARCH ON OSH!

Even though Babur really liked Samarkand, he was happy to be back home, because there were many things he liked to do in Fergana, too. For example, he liked riding his white pony whom he called Gul because gul means rose and Babur liked roses.

He also liked to wrestle and shoot arrows and fight with a sword. He liked to hear stories about his ancestors, Temur and Chenghis Khan, and about the grand cities of Samarkand and Bukhara and Kabul, and faraway countries like China and Persia and Hindustan.

Babur's gang had his two best friends, Sultan Ali and Buri, and his sister Khanzada. Mostly, they would play at being hunters and soldiers, or tigers and buzzards. But some days, when the fun was bubbling out of Babur from his toes out through his nose, he would say, "Today, we march on Osh!", and everybody would cheer.

15

What was so special about Osh? Well, for one thing, it had a very pretty mosque. And by the side of the mosque was a playful little river that flowed right down into a meadow full of soft green grass and low, leafy trees. It was the kind of place that just makes you want to stop and have a picnic, then and there.

Almost every day, a traveller or two would pass by here. They would be tired and dusty and their feet would be hurting from walking. When they saw the river, they would smile. They would gulp down a long cool drink of water, and as the sun dried the water on their lips, they would take off their boots, and lie down on the soft grass, and close their eyes and say, Aah!

Soon, they would be snoring, breathing in and out and in and out . . . and dreaming of dinner.

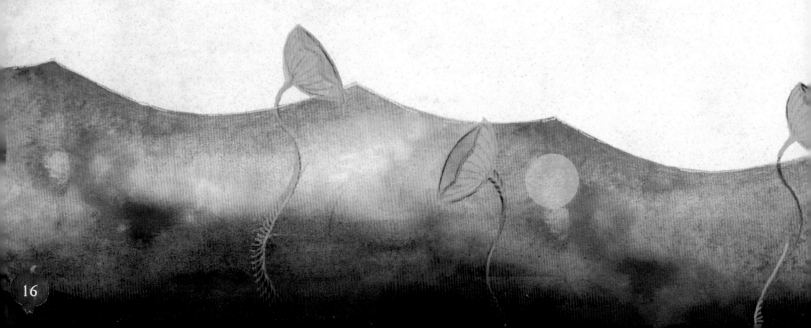

And all this while, Babur and his gang were hiding in a bush, pressing their hands on their mouths to hold in their giggles. When the travellers were fast asleep, the gang would tip-toe tip-toe down to the river, and they would scoop ice water into their little buckets, and they would hurry-scurry to the sleeping travellers and then

SPLASH!

they would pour the water all over their heads!

Then, as the men shook themselves like wet dogs and began to yell, Babur and Sultan Ali and Buri and Khanzada would run off into the hills, laughing until their stomachs hurt.

A BAD THING HAPPENS

So Babur kept growing, as we all tend to do, and his days were full of happiness and his nights were full of story. And then, when Babur was twelve years old, a very bad thing happened.

Umar Shaikh had gone to look at his pigeons. You see, Umar Shaikh liked three things best: to eat, to laugh, and to keep pigeons as pets. Umar Shaikh had so many pet pigeons, in fact, that he had built a special house for them in his palace, high up as a minaret right next to a cliff. One day, Umar Shaikh was up in his pigeon house feeding his birds, when the walls began to shudder and shiver behind him, and the floor began to jiggle and joggle beneath him, and the whole room went

CLATTER-BOOM!

— and Umar Shaikh went falling down and down and down the cliff, and when he fell, he broke his head.

Sometimes, when very bad things happen, there is nothing you can do but cry. So that is what Babur did.

19

Days went by and Babur became sadder and sadder still, and the sadness made him angry and grumpy and all twisted up, like a broken toy or a bad dream.

"Go away!" he said to Sultan Ali, when Sultan Ali brought him a brand new bow-and-arrow set to play with.

"Go away!" he said to Buri, when Buri brought him a freshly-cut mirtimuri melon, sweet as honey.

"Go away!" he said to Khanzada, who only wanted to sit in his room with him. When everyone had gone away and Babur was alone, he walked moodily through the palace corridors. He dragged his feet and kicked the floor. He pulled at a loose string on his jacket. He plucked the feather from his turban and tore it into small pieces.

"Babur!"

"What?" He recognised the voice but did not turn.

"Babur? Stop, come here!"

"Oh why, Nene!" He threw his arms in the air.
"I want to be alone!"

Babur's grandmother looked at him and replied gently,
"Be careful what you want, my Babur."

"I want everyone to go away!"

"Babur, Baboor. How I wish you could be a child longer. But Babur, dry your eyes. You are King now, and there are many things you have to do."

"But I don't want to be King! I want to be me! I want my father to be King. My father . . ." Tears filled Babur's eyes. Nene walked quickly towards him and pulled him into a long and deep hug. "Oh Babur, how I wish you could stay my Little Tiger always. I know how much it hurts in your stomach, I know my darling boy. But hush. You are King now, and danger is already knocking at your door."

"Danger?" Babur sniffled "But Nene, I am King. Nothing is dangerous for Kings."

"One thing is, Babur. It is very dangerous for a King to be without a Kingdom. And listen to me carefully: you are a King but you are also a small boy. Many who are bigger and older will think they can grab your Kingdom easily. Only today, I heard that Hasan Yaqub plots to overthrow you."

"What? Hasan Yaqub? But . . . but why? He taught me leap-frogging. We play polo together. He's really good, too. I always choose him for my team. Why would he . . ."

"Babur, a man can be good at polo and still be bad at heart. Don't waste time. Gather your friends and go find him. He's out hunting now and thinks you don't know what he's planning. Or maybe he thinks you do know, but are scared to act."

"Scared! Me?" The tears in Babur's eyes vanished. Instead, there came a red rage. "I'll show him who's scared!" He turned to run.

"And Babur?"

"What Nene? I must hurry!"

"Yes, but take this first. This is your father's sword: it will protect you."

Babur took the sword in both hands. Its handle was gold and its blade was very long, and very thin, and very sharp. "Thank you, Nene," he said, softly, and turned to go again.

"Babur, one more thing!"

"Oh what Nene! Hasan Yaqub will run away!"

"Hasan Yaqub will run nowhere that you cannot catch him. But here, put this feather back in your turban before you go. You know, your great-great-*great*-grandfather Temur was the first to wear one. It means you are strong, like him, so be proud of it, and it will guide you."

Babur gathered his friends and then he called Qasim Beg, who was the best soldier in his army. "Grab your sharpest swords and get on your horses," said Qasim Beg. "While that stinking Hasan Yaqub is hunting deer, *we* will hunt him."

They galloped off into the forest, but when they reached the hunting ground, it was empty. "Look at that" said Qasim Beg, with a grin, "they've left the deer half-roasted. Hasan Yaqub must have heard us coming and run away!"

"Coward that he is," said Babur, and he waved his sword in the air. It made a swishing-shwooshing sound, like ocean waves do when they are terribly angry.

"My sword and I have never seen a real battle," thought Babur. *"But soon, I suppose, we shall."* The thought scared him a little, and a little, it excited him.

But little did he know: soon would be a long, long time coming.

ONE NIGHT IN SAMARKAND

Three years!" Babur announced to the room. "Three full years!"

"Yes," said Nene.

"Yes," nodded Sultan Ali.

"Yes," Buri got up and yawned a loud yawn.

"Long years."

"Yes, well . . ."

"BO-ring years."

"Yes, but . . ."

"Three years and what have I done? One day, I hear my uncles want my throne. Next day, I hear my father's friends are no longer my friends."

"Babur, listen . . ."

"And every day I am told: Be careful what you eat, it may be poisoned." He threw a fat almond into the air and caught it with his teeth. "Be careful what you eat with, even your *spoon* may be poisoned. Always be careful and pray to God that he protects you. But how long, how long Nene, will God protect me if I do not fight for myself?"

Nobody spoke. Babur chewed another almond. "I have such a small kingdom" he said, thoughtfully, "but even so, I can't keep it safe. What must I do?"

"Guard your throne, Padishah," said the burly Qambar Ali.

"Watch your enemies, Babur," said Sultan Ali, sternly.

But Babur's grandmother shook her head. "A small kingdom will always be unsafe, Babur. What you need is —"

"A big kingdom!" said Babur. "You're *right*, Nene. That's the only way people will stop attacking me. When they see how strong I am. And I know how to make it bigger, too." His eyes glittered with excitement. "I'm going to capture Samarkand!"

Now you must be thinking, "That's not very nice. Why does Babur want to capture his Uncle's palace?" But that's because you don't know the whole story. You see, Samarkand had already been captured from Babur's Uncle. It was now ruled by the ruthless Shaibani Khan.

Shaibani Khan was not a good ruler. He had a terrible temper and was always chopping off people's heads, so nobody liked him. He also had beady eyes and his skin was full of little holes, as if it were being eaten up by woodworms. That's why Babur called him the Woodworm King.

The very next day, Babur's army set out for the great city of Samarkand. The soldiers sang songs of war, and Babur rode right in front, his sword shining like the sun. Even Gul and all the other horses wore armour: red and gold on their backs, and special helmets on their faces.

Clank and thump and stomp we march!
Clang and thud and stamp we march!
But Samarkand is far away,
You cannot reach it in a day!
So on we march and
Long we march!
Clank and thump!
Clang and thud!
Stamp and stomp!
And on we march!

Babur and his army passed many forts and villages on their way, and they conquered all of them. Every day, Babur became King of a new place. Finally, after many days, they reached the Iron Gate of Samarkand.

The Iron Gate was even bigger than Babur remembered. Tall as a giant. Thick as a jungle. And the stone wall! You could walk and walk ten thousand steps and still the wall wouldn't end.

"How will we get inside," thought Babur. *"It's so, so . . . SO big."*

But Babur didn't say this out loud, because he didn't want his soldiers to worry. "Make a circle around the fort," he ordered them instead. "Don't let anyone get out!"

"But now what? They can't come out, but we can't go in either."

Babur sat down on a rock and began to think.

He thought big thoughts and he thought small thoughts.
He thought clear thoughts and he thought mad thoughts.
He thought long thoughts till the day turned dark.
But all he could think was a question mark . . .
Till he finally thought, with a grin on his mouth:
*"Well I **think** now I've thought up a plan!"*

The next night, if you happened to live just outside Samarkand and
went out to play after dinner, you would have seen a strange sight.
At first, you might have thought black panthers were prowling ahead
of you. But if you looked closer, you'd see it was Babur and his men.
They were covered in black cloth, to look like the night, and they were
creeping softly towards Samarkand, on their hands and knees.

"Shh!" said Babur, "We walk like ghosts tonight. Understand?
Samarkand is asleep. The Woodworm King is snoring. So hush!"

Soft and gentle Babur crept. Two hundred men
followed. And if you squeezed your eyes and looked
very close, you would see that they carried ladders.

That's right: ladders. That was Babur's plan.

As soon as the soldiers reached the city walls, they put up their ladders and began to climb. Up they went, quiet and quick like ants. Up and up and whoop! they jumped into Samarkand.

"Quick, before the guards wake up, let's go let's go!" Babur whispered. No sooner had he said this, Buri called out "Babur! Watch out, there's one behind you, he's going to call the others!"

Like a tiger, Babur pounced on the guard. He put one hand on his mouth, and held a sharp chaqu to his throat. "Tell me," he said with a big smile, "how do you like your new King?"

While all this was going on, Shaibani Khan was fast asleep in the palace, snoring so loudly that his bed sheets billowed around him, like the sails of a ship. Suddenly the door flew open and his minister came charging in. "Padishah, Padishah! Babur and his army have taken the city!"

When Shaibani Khan understood what had happened, he got so scared that he picked up his pyjamas, jumped out of the window, and ran for his life!

And that is how, when he was fifteen, Babur became King of Samarkand, and all the people shouted on the streets, "Long live Babur! Long live the Little Tiger!"

IT'S GOOD TO BE KING

Babur spent many happy days in Samarkand. He ate roast chicken for breakfast, and ice-lollies for dinner. He had picnics in all the pretty gardens, and played polo in the green meadows. He held a melon-eating competition and came first. To be King of Samarkand, he felt, was better than to be King of All the World.

But sometimes even the greatest King has bad luck.

One day, a messenger came charging into the palace. He was dry with dust and wet with sweat. In his hand, he carried a letter. "Padishah!" cried the messenger, and fell to the floor.

The letter was from Babur's grandmother. All it said was: *Your enemies are attacking Fergana. Come at once.*

Of course, Babur left immediately to save his Nene. But the slippery-slimy Shaibani Khan, the Woodworm King, had been lurking outside Samarkand, waiting for just such a chance. Quickly, he snuck back in, slammed the gates, and locked the palace doors. Now Babur was no longer King of Samarkand.

To make matters worse, when Babur reached Fergana, he found that his enemies had already captured his home. Now Babur was no longer King of Fergana, either.

"Buri! Sultan Ali! Qambar Ali! We have to attack — my mother and Nene are locked up in Fergana. And Khanzada's all alone in Samarkand! I have to rescue them, come, now!"

Babur jumped on Gul and looked down at his friends. But all three shook their heads. "Which way will you go, Babur?" asked Buri, in a sad voice.

"Both ways! First I'll take back Fergana, then I'll attack Samarkand, and then I'll have both in my pocket before the night is over. And if you don't come with me, you are no more my friend!"

But Qambar Ali caught hold of Gul's reins and said, "Padishah, no. I have fought many battles and I have always been loyal to your father and to you. But listen to me, my King, you need two armies now and you barely have one. If you fight tonight, you will not live tomorrow."

"I will! With no one but Gul, if that's how it is, I will!" Babur snatched at his sword.

"You will not. Listen to me: Khanzada is alone in Samarkand with Old Woodworm, it's true. But he will not dare harm her, as long as he knows you are alive."

"He's right, Babur," said Sultan Ali. "We must wait and think of another plan. That is what your Nene would say, and you know she's always right."

Tears filled Babur's eyes, but he listened to his friends. He had lost Fergana and he had lost Samarkand. He had lost his Nene and his mother and his sister. He was no more Babur the King, he was only Babur the Boy. And there was nothing he could do about it.

THE VAGABOND

atch some dust, slowpokes!" Babur shouted as he galloped past Buri and Sultan Ali. The sound of Gul's hooves thundered in their ears. Babur turned in his saddle and saw that Buri was waving at him. Babur waved back and shouted again, "Ha-ha! If you go any slower, you'll go backwards!"

Too late, he realised his friend wasn't waving, he was pointing. Babur's saddle was loose. With a shout of surprise he fell backwards, off Gul, on the ground, bang on his head.

Anyone who falls on their head like that will cry in pain. But Babur jumped up as if he'd landed on a fat cushion instead of a rock. In a moment, he was back on his horse, and his small group of vagabonds continued down to the village below the mountain.

Though Babur had no kingdom, no army, no friends except the few men who believed in him, he was still the great-great-*great*-grandson of Temur the Great and Chenghis Khan, and the village headman greeted him with a bow. "Babur, you are welcome," he said. "Stay with me in my home, and tonight we shall eat our fattest sheep."

That night, they sat around the bukhari and ate without speaking. Babur and his men were cold and hungry after days of riding through the winter, and the bubbling stew heated them up, from their stomachs to their toes. Finally, slurping down the last of the gravy in his bowl, Babur cried, "Aah! Now *that* is a meal for a King! What do you say, boys, shall we raid Samarkand tonight?"

"Yes! Yes!" they shouted, banging their spoons on their plates. "Hail to the Padishah! Samarkand shall fall!"

As the voices grew louder, Babur saw a small shadow moving in the dark. He leaped up, his hand reaching for his sword. "Who's that? Stop!"

The shouting stopped, and everyone turned to stare. Very slowly, the shadow came closer and they saw that it was an old woman, bent like a banana. "All hail the Padishah," she said in a tiny voice, and waved her stick in the air with a flourish.

"You touch my heart, Grandmother," said Babur, with a big grin.

"And you touch mine, little Babur. Show me your face, let me put it in my mind forever." Babur bent down and the old woman held him by his chin, examining every inch of his face with great concentration. Finally, she let him go. "Do you know, little Babur, how old I am?"

"Not a day older than the spring, Grandmother!"

"You know how to flatter, Little Tiger," she laughed, "But I am one hundred and eleven years old. So old that I remember your great-great-*great*-grandfather, Temur. Do you know, I went with his army when he conquered Hindustan."

"With Temur himself! Really, Grandmother?"

"Yes, little Babur. And I see in your eyes the same flame that burned in his. Samarkand will surely be yours."

"*And then, maybe even Hindustan?*" said Babur, but he said it to himself. The idea was so enormous, he could hardly bear to speak it out loud.

The next day, Babur and his gang went exploring. There were hills all around the village, with little paths leading off into thick forests.

They had walked a long while, munching
on fruits from the trees and making jokes,
when Buri said, "Does anyone know how
we'll get back?"

Everyone stopped and looked at each other. "It seems," said Buri, "that we are lost."

"Oh how you worry!" Babur laughed. "Look, there's a cow. All we have to do is follow her, she'll take us back, I'm sure."

As he pointed, the cow trotted down a narrow path and they all ran to follow it. Every so often, Qambar Ali would call out in his booming voice, "At any cost, I hope the cow isn't lost!" — and then he would laugh cheerfully at his own joke.

But the cow kept going, turning steeply this way and that, until everyone became very confused. And then, because sometimes life is just a big surprise, the cow turned a corner and banged straight into Nene, walking hand-in-hand with Babur's mother.

"Nene!" Babur ran and wrapped his grandmother in a big hug. "Aaneh!" he kissed his mother. "Nene!" again, and then "Aaneh!" — until finally he held them both in one giant tiger's embrace, and they all three began to cry with happiness.

"Oh my darling," they kissed him on both cheeks, two times each.

"How tall you've grown!"

"I wanted to rescue you. I couldn't. I'm sorry!"

"Sorry!" said Nene. "Why be sorry? You may be a Big Tiger now, but I'm the tiger's grandmother, don't forget. I should hope I can rescue myself! And look who else I've brought with me!"

Now she turned and a whole procession walked up behind her. All Babur's friends and cousins who'd been trapped in Fergana had escaped.

Babur looked embarrassed. "But I'm not a Tiger any more, Nene. I'm not a King, even. I'm just a . . . a Vagabond."

"Is that so? And don't vagabonds have parties to welcome their mothers and grandmothers?"

While Babur was still trying to reply, Qambar Ali took a step forward and said in a most sober way, "Ladies, a gala feast at any cost, unless that silly cow is lost!" — and everyone burst out laughing.

A VERY COLD WINTER

When you really want something, like your birthday, or a bicycle, or chocolate ice cream, it's very hard to think of anything else. That's how it was with Babur, too. He wanted — he really, really, *really* wanted — to be King of Samarkand. And he could think of nothing else.

But birthdays come, bicycles can be bought, and sometimes, when you're lucky, you'll find ice cream hidden in the back of the freezer. This almost never happens with Kingdoms. Babur and his friends were eager to capture Samarkand, but they didn't have an army. They didn't have weapons. They didn't have homes, or tents, or enough horses. They wandered in the mountains, hunting for food and sleeping on rocks. And when the winter came, they found they didn't even have proper shoes.

Mountain winters are cold. The roads and the trees are all covered with snow, and if your shoes have holes in them, as Babur and his friends' shoes did, then the snow gets in and wets your socks and your toes, and you are squelchy and cold for days. If you're lucky enough to get soup, you have to drink it up immediately, or it turns to ice in the bowl. At night, a wind roars in the sky, louder than ten tigers and full of nightmares.

On one such night, Babur and his friends were sitting huddled around the cold ashes of their campfire. The little wood they had, had finished, and now there was neither warmth nor light to cheer them. Worse, tonight they had only found one tiny cave, hardly big enough for anyone to sleep in. Everyone had offered the cave to Babur, because Babur was the leader, but he had refused. "Do you really think I could sleep inside, knowing that you're all shivering out here? I may not be King any more, but I do have my honour."

This was very noble of Babur, but it didn't make him or his friends any less cold. They huddled together, rubbing themselves for heat, too tired and shivery to even talk. But then, as the night grew darker and the wind grew louder, and their feet grew stiffer and their stomachs growled, Buri cried out in anger, "This is terrible!"

"I know," said Babur. "I'm sorry that because of me —"

"It's cold and wet and I am hungry!"

"I am, too. But look, when we capture Samarkand . . ."

"Oh Samarkand, Samarkand — to hell with Samarkand! I just want a bed. I would give ten Samarkands for one blanket and a pillow!"

"But you know my mind is set on Samarkand."

"Well in that case," said Buri, quietly but firmly, "I think it is time you changed your mind."

Kings fight wars and rule empires. But the most important thing they do is listen to good advice. Babur was not yet twenty-five and he was poor and he had no Kingdom, but at heart he was a King. So, though Buri's

words hurt him and he didn't want to, at all, let go of Samarkand, he realised that he must.

The next day, a pale yellow sun rose gingerly into the frosty sky. Babur and his men shook themselves to remove the snow on their coats, and stamped their feet on the ground, and tried not to think about breakfast (because there wasn't any), and Babur made an announcement.

"Let us leave this place, my friends. It is full of snow and dead trees and nothing else. Let us go, I say, to Kabul, which is warm and rich with fruit and rivers. Let us go today itself. Let us go now!"

At this, the men shouted with happiness and, not waiting a minute longer, they began to race southwards to the great city of the Afghans, Kabul.

KHUSRAU SHAH GETS A FRIGHT

Kabul is very far from Fergana, across the steep and snowy Hindu Kush mountains, and it takes months of climbing and riding and walking to get there. To go so far from home to an unknown place, not knowing what you will find there, would scare anybody. But Babur wasn't particularly scared, and that was so because of three reasons:

First of all, Babur's mother went with him, and there is nothing quite like a mother to make you feel less afraid.

Second of all, Babur's cheeks had finally begun to feel the tickle of a beard and he had started shaving. This made him feel quite grown-up and daring.

Third of all, Kabul was ruled by a rather silly man called Muqim Beg, who only liked to have parties and didn't care at all whether the people of Kabul were happy or not. Still, Muqim Beg was only empty-headed; his governors in other parts of Afghanistan were crafty and mean.

The worst of these governors was Khusrau Shah, a cruel man with thin lips and hollow cheeks, who took everything good and precious for himself and hated to share. Everywhere that Babur went, villagers and soldiers and noblemen told him what evil things Khusrau Shah had done, and to all these people Babur said: "Then join me, and I will be a good King, and you will be happy."

So Babur kept walking towards Kabul, and every day more and more soldiers came

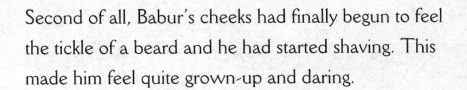

to him, until almost all of Khusrau Shah's men had joined Babur's small army. Finally, Khusrau Shah himself sent a messenger to Babur.

Babur laughed when the messenger had gone. "Ha! Did you hear that? The wily dog, Khusrau Shah says it will be an 'honour to meet me'. I wonder what more lies he plans to tell when he comes."

The next day, Babur laid out his best carpet under a shady tree and sat down. He kept a bowl-full of sugared almonds next to him, and when Khusrau Shah arrived, he began to eat them one by one, smacking his lips with pleasure. But, though Khusrau Shah's eyes darted longingly towards the bowl, Babur didn't offer him any, and nor did Khusrau Shah dare to ask.

"Welcome, Padishah," said Khusrau Shah, bowing deep and long. "I hope you are enjoying this beautiful country?"

"Why thank you, Khusrau Shah. How nice of you to come and meet me. Though I must say, your people have already made my stay very comfortable!"

With these words, Babur turned and waved at the great crowd of soldiers behind him, all from poor Khusrau Shah's army.

"These wastrels and villains?" Khusrau Shah sneered. "These rogues and rapscallions? I would not place my faith in them, Padishah.

These scamps have left me four times already — and each time they have come back."

"Is that so?" said Babur. He was surprised and worried by this, but he did not let it show. "Is that so," he said again. "Well, my dear Khusrau Shah, since you have advised me not to trust these men, let me advise you not to trust *those*, either." Now Babur pointed at the few soldiers who had come with Khusrau Shah. Having seen their friends standing behind Babur, all of them were changing sides too!

You should have seen Khusrau Shah's face. His eyes popped right out of his head, and his cheeks turned bright purple with embarrassment and rage. But what could he do? With great effort, Khusrau Shah twisted his lips into a crooked smile. "Padishah," he said, bowing once again, "I am glad to have met you, but now I think I must go home."

"I think so too, my dear Khusrau Shah," said Babur, doing his best not to smile too gleefully.

Khusrau Shah tried to look very dignified as he walked away, but then he tripped on a piece of wood and fell on his face. At this, Babur couldn't help himself any more, and he burst out laughing.

Forgetting all about dignity, Khusrau Shah hurried off and never showed his face in Afghanistan again.

After this, word of Babur's strength and popularity spread through the country. People said to each other:

Did you hear how Babur won?
He did not battle, brawl or fight,
He only sat under a tree
And gave old Khusrau Shah a fright!

Oh Babur is a clever lad!
Who wants to scrap and strife and shout,
When you can sit under a tree
And have your foe be routed out?

By the time Babur and his army reached Kabul, silly old Muqim Beg was trembling like jelly, and before Babur had even knocked at the city gates, Muqim Beg had run away.

Once more, Babur was King, and to be King of Kabul, he found, was almost better than being King of Samarkand.

53

A DOZEN WORLDS IN ONE

The first thing Babur did after becoming King of Kabul was to give his mother the best rooms in the palace, and lots of books to read and the finest clothes to wear.

The next thing he did was to go out exploring. Luckily, Kabul was the perfect kind of Kingdom to go exploring in. Should he ride off one morning, Babur might soon reach hot, sandy deserts, where camels chomped on dry thorns and the wind could boil water. And then, should he ride another two hours, he would be up a craggy mountain, so cold that its thick snow never melted.

But even if he rode nowhere, Babur only had to open the gates of his palace to reach a dozen different worlds at once.

When you and I step out of our homes, we are used to seeing one or two kinds of people, and hearing one or two kinds of languages, and that is how it is in most towns. But Kabul was no ordinary town. Kabul was a place of hubbub-and-hustle and bluster-and-bustle. Kabul was, in fact, a Hub of International Trade.

You see, if you and I wanted to be International Traders today, what we would do is, we'd buy a lot of tea, or mangoes, or jujubes, and we'd pack them in cartons, and we'd stack them all up in a big ship, and the ship would sail off to New York or Rotterdam or Jakarta, where people would buy all these great things.

But if you wanted to be an International Trader in Babur's time, well, things were a little different. First, you would pack up all your silk cloth or your black pepper or your rock sugar and load it up into wagons that were pulled by steady horses or camels. These lines of wagons were called caravans, and once you had your caravan ready, you would clamber up a steady horse or camel yourself, and head off to a faraway market.

"Come and see my sheep's wool,
soft as a cloud!"
"Come and taste my cardamom,
it really does me proud!"
"Come and see this lamp of gold —"
"See, oh see my silken robes!"
"Come and see what all we've got!
Before it gets all sold!"

减价?
(Discount?)

यह कितने
का है?
(How much is this?)

57

More often than not, that faraway market was in Kabul.

Which is why Babur only had to walk out, and he would find merchants from hilly Fergana and gleaming Samarkand, from Badakhshan and Bukhara and even from Balkh, from Turkey and China and Iraq and beyond, and of course, of course, from Hindustan.

These shopkeepers and bookmakers, apprentice boys and girls, would all be calling out and bargaining, in Arabic or Persian, Turkish, Mongolian, Pashai and Parachi, Hindi, Afghani, and a dozen old languages more. And if you stood there long enough, as Babur often did, you would begin to understand, one word after another, and soon you would be part of all the buying and selling and bargaining going on around you.

Babur enjoyed all this very much, and he often found new and exciting things to buy. He liked the little nuts called jalghozas, which were so difficult to take out of their shells but so delicious to eat. He tasted sugar cane for the first time, and he liked the sticky, juicy plant so much that he had a whole lot grown in his favourite garden, the Bagh-e-Wafa. He also planted a cherry tree here and a banana tree, and watered them every day, till they grew big and heavy with fat red cherries and soft yellow bananas that everyone loved to eat, especially Gul.

But just as Babur was discovering all these things, and just as he was planning to bring his Nene here and show her all he'd seen, his mother fell ill. Her fever was hot and high, and though the doctors gave her all kinds of medicines and ice-cold watermelon, too, it wouldn't come down. One day, she closed her eyes and never woke up again. Then, just a few days later, Babur got a letter telling him his Nene was too old to live any more.

Suddenly, Babur was very alone. He spent more and more time in his garden, sitting at the very centre of the Bagh-e-Wafa on a little hill, with four beds of flowers and a stream flowing down it. Babur liked being here, among the roses and tulips, watching the snowy mountains up ahead and the fruit trees down below. Sometimes, to make him feel better, people would come and show him strange new animals. One day, it was a bird as big as a dog, with feathers in five bright colours, which they called a Tragopan. Another day, they brought him a furry little thing that looked just like a fox. But, the minute it was set free, it spread out its wings, flapped them once or twice like an eagle, and flew off into the air.

Then, one day, they brought him not a strange animal, but a young woman, thin and pale, who walked nervously behind a soldier.

"Who are you?" asked Babur, kindly. When the young woman didn't answer, he turned and raised his eyebrows at the soldier.

He came close to Babur and whispered a word in his ear. "Khanzada!" Babur shouted, jumping up and rushing to his sister. "Khanzada! I cannot believe it is you!"

But Khanzada did not smile and only looked more pale and confused. "Do you not know who I am?" asked Babur. She was staring up at his face, frowning in a confused way. "You don't recognise me!" Babur laughed. "Oh Khanzada. Wait, this will remind you." Babur reached for his sword and waved it in a big circle above their heads. "Come," he cried, "today, shall we march on Osh?"

At this, the worry vanished from Khanzada's face. "It's the beard!" she said, slapping her forehead. "How silly that I didn't recognise you."

"Aah, but it *has* been ten years," said Babur, folding his arms around his sister. "How I wanted to come and rescue you from that —"

"Shaibani Khan."

"That Woodworm King!" Babur made a disgusted face. "That stinky scoundrel! Just his name gives me indigestion!" Babur was beginning to yell in anger, but then he saw the pale look return to his sister's face and he stopped. You see, though it is important for a King to be strong, it is even more important for a King to understand what other people need, especially those who are weak or injured or sad. So, Babur lowered his voice and said, "I'm sorry."

"No Babur, don't blame yourself. What could you have done, only a little boy then? And Shaibani . . . the Woodworm King, he was never cruel to me. He married me, and I was comfortable, though very alone. And now that he has died in battle, I am free. And you, little brother," she ended, with a twinkle in her eye, "*you* are free to pamper me as never before!"

And because Babur was King and could do whatever he wanted, so, indeed, it was.

GUL HAS AN IDEA

The years passed, and Babur found more and more things to enjoy in Kabul, and made more and more friends to enjoy them with. Like Umar Shaikh, his father, Babur would have big parties, and everyone would eat and drink and dance till late at night. That grizzly old soldier, Qasim Beg, liked to sing, though his voice was like a wild boar gargling. Everyone would put their fingers in their ears and scrunch up their noses, but Qasim Beg paid no attention and continued singing. And Babur never told him to stop, because Qasim Beg was his friend, and a loyal and brave friend he was, too.

As Babur grew older, he married a girl called Maham, and then he had a son. He called the baby Humayun, because Humayun means Good Luck, and good luck is always important, and often necessary. Then, he held a grand feast to celebrate.

All the noblemen and noblewomen of Kabul came to the feast, and they brought gifts of silver coins, which they piled up in the garden until there was a little silver-coin mountain, and Babur thanked everybody, and they all joined the chorus of Qasim Beg's songs, and the food was delicious and the guests kept coming and the party kept going, until the night had ended and it was dawn.

Afterwards, Babur got on Gul and went riding to an empty meadow. The sun was just rising, and it lit up the yellow clover flowers all around, making them shine buttery-gold. A small river gurgled nearby and birds chirruped. Babur thought he had never seen a bluer sky, or felt a cooler breeze, or had a happier feeling. "Well, Gul," he said, patting the old mare's neck, "it seems that we have found a place to live in, happily ever after."

Gul snorted loudly.

"What?" asked Babur, surprised. "Don't tell me you want to go off and have more adventures?"

At this, Gul whinnied and raised her front legs in the air, as if preparing to charge off into the horizon.

"Settle down, girl, settle down!" Babur shouted, laughing and holding on to his turban with one hand. "But maybe you are right. Maybe it is time . . ."

He didn't say what it was time for, but a long-ago thought began to whirr once again, very softly, in his mind.

And many years later, just like that, the whirr turned into a *click*.

Just like that? Well, maybe not. What happened was this:

You already know how Babur liked to go exploring. When Humayun was old enough to ride, Babur gave him Gul's young son, a fine black pony called Guldobara, and took them both exploring, too. Further and further they went, finding new kinds of people and fruits and animals, and the world seemed endless and grand. One day, when Humayun was seventeen years old, Babur called him to his court and said, "My son, I have a new adventure for you, unlike anything you have dreamed of. Tell me, are you game?"

"Of course, Padishah! When am I not?"

"We go in search of a new beast, a creature of dreams. It is neither cow nor elephant, though it eats grass and makes the earth shake when it runs. Its skin is armour and its nose a deadly spear. They call it Rhino Saurus, and I am itching to see it."

"I will be ready to ride at dawn, Padishah," said Humayun, grinning from ear to ear.

So off they set, Babur and Humayun, and with them a small army of ten thousand men, all eager for a sight of this weird new animal. They walked south and east to the forests of Peshawar, where, it was said, the Rhino Saurus lived.

One day, as they marched, there was a big commotion behind them, and with cries of "Padishah! Padishah!" two men on a rickety wagon came tumbling forward. When they reached Babur, both men hopped to the ground and bowed low. "Padishah," said the smaller of the two, "my name is Ali-Quli and this is my assistant Mustafa. We come from Istanbul and we bring you a miracle."

"A miracle?" asked Babur, raising his eyebrows. "What fun. Let's see it?"

Ali-Quli gestured to Mustafa, who hurried to the back of their wagon and came back carrying a long, thin metal pipe.

"What's this?" asked Babur.

"This, Padishah, is a weapon to conquer the world!" said Ali-Quli in a dramatic voice, spreading his arms to the sky.

"This!" said Babur, and he couldn't help laughing. "My dear Ali-Quli, this is a pipe. It has no sharp edge, no pricking point, and it is far too heavy to throw. You could hit someone on the head with it, but that miracle is performed daily by children armed with sticks!"

"But Padishah . . ."

"Ali-Quli, I am pleased you came so far and I see you are a good man. But I'm afraid you've misjudged this 'weapon', old fellow. Come, come, don't worry. Follow us to the Rhino Saurus. Now *that* promises to be a real wonder."

So off they went, with poor Ali-Quli and Mustafa in tow, and the next day they were in the forests of Peshawar, creeping softly one by one, eyes wide open and hearts a-thump.

And then, with a hot snort and long harrumph . . . there it was! Oh what a creature!

Its face was dark as thunder,
Its legs were thick as trees,
And on its nose there was a spike
That made the soldiers freeze!

The first to react was Guldobara. With a squeak of fear, he began running backwards, which is a funny sight when a horse does it, but nobody laughed because they were all very scared themselves. The Rhino Saurus rubbed its front leg on the ground. It lowered its head and glowered at them with glinting eyes.

"It's going to charge," whispered Babur to himself. He turned to warn his men and saw Ali-Quli and Mustafa hurrying forward, carrying their metal pipes in their hands. "Fools," said Babur as they approached, "run back!"

But Ali-Quli paid no attention. Instead, he raised the metal pipe to his chest and began fiddling with its handle. For a second, they stared at each other: Babur at Ali-Quli, Ali-Quli at the Rhino Saurus, and the Rhino Saurus at Babur's army.

There was a small click.

And then, there was a loud BOOM!

And it was as if a bit of the sun had exploded before them. With a hop and a yelp, the Rhino Saurus turned and fled. The soldiers looked at each other with open mouths. Babur turned to Ali-Quli.

"Forgive me," he said. "I doubted you. But that . . . that is truly a miracle no man has seen before. What do you call it, Ustad?"

"It is called a matchlock-gun, Padishah. But if you like this, just wait till you see the cannon-taups I have. Those throw out giant balls of fire. And before you ask: my wagon is full of them." .

THE WORLD ACROSS THE RIVER

Since nobody wanted to look for Rhino Sauruses any more, Babur decided to go exploring around Peshawar instead. Soon, he reached a river, bigger and more blue than any he had ever seen. This was the great Indus, and on its other side was Hindustan.

Babur stood by the river for a long time, looking at the endless tumbling water and imagining all the rich and wonderful things across, and when he had stood there long enough he turned, because now he had made up his mind.

That night, Babur called his most loyal soldiers to his tent. There was Qasim Beg and Sultan Ali and Buri of old; and there was Hindu Beg, and Ustad Ali-Quli and Muhammad Ali Jang-Jang, who were new; and of course there was Humayun.

"My friends, my son," said Babur, when everyone had sat down, "sometimes some things are meant to be, or so it seems to me. Just look how, out of nowhere, Ustad Ali-Quli brought us miracle matchlock guns. And look how here we are, on the very brink of Hindustan. What an adventure it will be, will it not, if we go forward and try to capture this fabulous land that none of us have seen except in our dreams?"

"But . . . it is too big and too hot," said Buri.

"The Sultan of Hindustan, Ibrahim Lodi, is too rich and too powerful," said Hindu Beg.

"His army has a hundred thousand men and three thousand elephants," said Humayun.

"But does he have even one of our guns?" Babur asked. "And does he have one drop of our courage? Why, if my Nene were here, she would not hesitate, so why do you? We have had many good times, all of us, we have drunk many nights and sung many songs, and seen many wonders. But shall we say, Oh that is enough? Shall we say, No more, no more? Is *that* the kind of explorers we are?"

"No, Padishah!" they chorused, "We want more, Padishah, we want more!" — and their voices rose loud in the night, so full of excitement that even the Rhino Sauruses in the jungle heard them, and wondered what was going on.

A LARGE ARMY AND A BIG SURPRISE

Now, before we get to Babur and his battle against Ibrahim Lodi, tell me this: Supposing there was just the one of you, and you had to fight ten people, how would you do it? You could, I suppose, try to fight all ten at once. And that would be very brave of you, but also very silly, because you would certainly lose.

But what if you could somehow turn all ten people into one person? Wouldn't that make things easier? Maybe, but how's that possible, you're asking, and you're right. It isn't. But even so, what you can do, if you're clever, is turn ten people into one person *at a time.*

You see, when Babur came to fight Ibrahim Lodi outside Panipat, he had ten thousand soldiers and Ibrahim Lodi had one hundred thousand. That means, for every *one* of Babur's soldiers, Ibrahim Lodi had ten. Even if you have taups and matchlock guns, one against ten isn't a good situation to be in.

So what did Babur do? Well, first he picked a good spot. The good spot was just outside Panipat, with the houses and other buildings to his right. To his left, he told his soldiers to dig deep ditches and cover them with branches. Next, he got hundreds of empty bullock-carts and tied them together with rope, so they became a long wooden chain.

He stretched this wooden chain between the houses and the ditches, and he told Ustad Ali-Quli and Mustafa to take their matchlock-guns and taups and stand behind the carts, where nobody could see them. Finally, he patted Humayun's back and said, "Now, my son, all we must do is wait."

What Babur had done, you see, was make a trap. A long, narrow trap, like a corridor, with houses on one side, ditches on the other, and gunmen hidden behind carts in the middle. When Ibrahim Lodi's men attacked, they had to squeeze between the houses and the ditches, because there just wasn't enough room for all of them to charge at once.

And you can imagine what happens when a hundred thousand men get squeezed into a narrow line. A hundred thousand men become ten thousand men at a time. Plus, everyone is confused and irritated.

And just as they're pushing and shouting, "Get out of my way! You're poking my eye!" there is a . . .

BOOM! BOOM-BLAST-BOOM!

. . . and everyone starts running helter-skelter, shouting "What's that! Run!" — and before you know it, the battle is won.

By lunchtime that day, Babur was the new King of Hindustan, riding to Delhi to claim his throne.

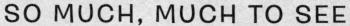

SO MUCH, MUCH TO SEE

To be King of Hindustan, Babur discovered, was very different from being King of Samarkand or King of Kabul. There was so much, much more to see.

In Delhi, Babur saw the dargah of Nizamuddin, where people came from all over to pray and sing. He saw the sparkling lake of Hauz Khas, and the great tower of Qutub, taller than any building on earth, so tall you had to tilt your head all the way to your back to see its top.

And he camped by the Yamuna river at night, when the moon and stars shone so bright in the water that it was as if a thousand candles floated upon it. And this was just Delhi, and Delhi was only the beginning of Hindustan.

Next, Babur went to Agra, where there was a great fort. Humayun was already there, and he came rushing to meet his father.

"Look, look, Padishah. Look what the Raja of Gwalior has given me!"

He held out a diamond, bigger than any in the world, shining so bright it made you blink. Babur took it in his hands and held it a moment. "I have heard of this gem, my son," he said. "They say this alone could buy the whole world all it wants for half a day."

"All it wants? Really?"

"Everything, yes. Sweets and shoes, paintbrushes and porcelain. Anything anyone can think of, for half a day."

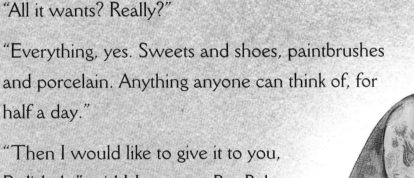

"Then I would like to give it to you, Padishah," said Humayun. But Babur smiled and shook his head and gave it right back.

Babur wasn't really interested in diamonds, you see. He liked lakes and gardens, and fruits and animals, and all kinds of flowers. And in Hindustan, he found, there were a million kinds of each.

There were mangoes, which Babur thought were almost as good as mirtimuri melons. He liked to squish them with both hands until they were all soft inside and he could slur-rrrup out the juice. He liked to drink the water of green coconuts, too, though he had never had any before and thought it tasted a bit like cheese. The yellow, star-shaped kamrak was sour in a good way: it made his tongue perk up and his eyes go round. The sangtara, round and orange, was pretty to look at, and it made delicious juice. And the soft petals of mahua flowers had a taste nobody can describe. But the jackfruit he didn't like. It was stinky, and it was ugly like sheep's intestines, and it made him crinkle his nose.

Every day, Babur found creatures he had never seen before. Langurs made him laugh, and the gilahri, as it ran quick-as-quick up a tree.

Nilgais were like deer
Except they were blue,
And peacocks were birds
That just never flew,
And he once met a stork
That swallowed a shoe!

Green parrots could talk
And cuckoos would sing
And frogs (like frogs everywhere)
Glubbered like drains.

Such were the creatures
He saw all around
But the strangest new creature
Babur ever found

Was the dog-faced chamgidar
The black-winged chamgidar
The flip-flapping bat
That flip-flapped and hung
Upside-down!

A DOG TO THE RESCUE

There are many good parts to being King. You can eat what you like and sleep when you want and have parties and go exploring whenever you feel like it. But there are some bad parts, too. You have to make sure everyone in your Kingdom is happy, and listen to everyone's problems, and not be impatient or unkind. There are always people in a Kingdom who do not like you, and you have to be watchful of them, and know who to trust.

One person who did not like Babur at all was Buwa, the mother of Sultan Ibrahim Lodi, whom Babur had defeated at Panipat. Buwa was angry that her son had lost and she wanted to hurt Babur. So, one day, she bribed the cook to put some poison in Babur's dinner.

That night, Babur had only taken a few bites of his food when he began to feel very ill. His stomach made grumbly noises and he got up and ran to the bathroom. But before he could even reach, he fell down and threw up all his food.

He was sitting in the corridor and holding his stomach when a small dog came by. The dog sniffed at the vomit and then, because that's just how dogs find out about things, he gave it a quick, experimental lick. And immediately, the small dog began to feel quite sick, too. He groaned and he whimpered and he lay down at Babur's feet.

"You poor dog," Babur whispered (because he was too weak to talk in his normal voice), "I'm afraid someone has tried a dirty trick on us both."

So Babur and the dog were taken to doctors, and they were both given medicine and told to rest, and they slept and slept for many days, until finally they felt better.

When Babur found out what had happened, he was very angry and he called Buwa to the palace. "How dare you!" he shouted when she came. "I shall have you thrown in the dark down-below dungeon. You will have nobody to poison there except the palace rats! You tried to kill me, you tried to kill the King! Answer, do you have no words?"

He waited for a reply, but Buwa said nothing. She stood tall and straight and silent and proud, and she did not look at all scared. And the more Babur looked at her, the more he remembered his Nene, who would have been so happy to come with him to Hindustan. Babur's eyes grew soft and his voice, too.

"Buwa," he said, "maybe I understand your silence. You did what you did for your son. Any mother would have done the same. I cannot hold this against you. Go now, and go in peace. But go far, where you cannot harm me, so we may both live long and happy . . . and apart."

ONE LAST EXPLORATION

abur was so happy not to have died from being poisoned that he decided to go on the longest exploration of his life.

He went to Chanderi, which is full of flowing streams and pretty lakes, and he went to Gwalior, where he bathed in a waterfall and saw a fort full of yellow ducks, and he rode through the forests of Bengal looking for tigers, and his tent was blown away by the rains in Bihar, and he swam across the Ganga in thirty strokes. And he would have gone on, further and beyond, but then Humayun fell terribly ill.

Babur galloped back to Agra and ran to his son's room. Humayun was so ill he couldn't even open his eyes. There was sweat on his face, and his body shivered, even though he was covered with blankets.

Babur sat by his son all day and all night for many weeks, but Humayun just wouldn't get well. Even the doctor looked scared and said, "Padishah, the illness is strong. I do not know what will cure it. Only God can help us now."

"In that case," said Babur, "I will talk to God."

That night, Babur climbed up to the roof of his palace. He looked long at the stars, milky dots in the sky, and he looked long at their mother, the moon. He thought of all that he had done and seen: of his father Umar Shaikh and the river in Osh, of Buri his best friend and Woodworm his worst enemy, of the gardens in Kabul and the mangoes in Hindustan. He remembered his battles and his parties, his Khanzada, his Nene, his Aaneh and Gul. And he smiled. He had been King of Three Places. What more could anyone want?

Babur raised his arms to the night sky and then he bowed down low. "My God, my Lord, my Padishah. You, who made this world for exploring. Heal my son. Take me."

His words floated away in the night breeze.

And then, because Babur was King and his heart was good, and because there is so much outside this world to explore, and because He had something even better up His Sleeve than a mirtimuri melon . . . God agreed.

The next morning, Humayun woke up and left his bed. He walked down the palace corridors into the court and stood before the empty throne. Then, with a soft prayer, he sat down upon it.

And so, as is the way of things, Humayun the Boy became Humayun the King.

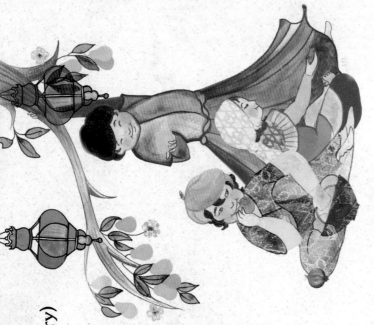

BABUR'S FAMILY TREE

CHENGHIS KHAN (13th century)
(Babur's great-great-great-great-great-great-great-great-great-great-grandfather)

— Phew!

Chagatai Khan

Moatukan

Yasuntao

Baraq Khan

Dua Khan

Esan-Buqa Khan

Tughluq-Timur Khan

Muhammad Khan

Sher-'ali Oghlan

Wais Khan

Yunus Khan who married Esan Daulat Khan, Babur's Nene

Qutlugh Nigar Khanim (Babur's mother)

AMIR TEMUR (1336-1405)
(Babur's great-great-great-grandfather)

Miranshah Mirza

Sultan Muhammad Mirza

Sultan Abusai'd Mirza

Umar Shaikh (Babur's father)

BABUR (1483-1530)

Humayun (1508-1556)

Akbar (1542-1605)

Jahangir (1569-1627)

Shahjahan (1592-1666)

Aurangzeb (1618-1707)

Bahadur Shah I (1643-1712)

Jahandar Shah (1661-1713)

Farrukhsiyar (1683-1719)

Muhammad Shah (1702-1748)

Ahmad Shah (1725-1775)

Alamgir II (1699-1759)

Shah Alam (1728-1806)

Akbar II (1760-1837)

Bahadur Shah II (1775-1862)

If you are afraid,
Don't do it,
If you are doing it,
Don't be afraid!

CHENGHIS KHAN

ABOUT SOME THINGS IN THIS BOOK

FERGANA

Fergana is where Babur was born on the 14th of February 1483. Fergana is also where he first became King when he was 12 years old. The town of Fergana is in a country called Uzbekistan, but the whole of Fergana Valley is spread out: a bit in Uzbekistan, a bit in Kyrgyzstan and the rest in Tajikistan.

SAMARKAND

Samarkand is a city in Uzbekistan, and if you go there, you'll see many of the grand buildings that Babur saw. A lot of these buildings were made by Temur, Babur's great-great-*great*-grandfather, and you'll find them around the Registan Square in the centre of Samarkand. Temur was once the King of Samarkand and is buried here in a tomb called the Gur-e-Amir. Samarkand was on the ancient Silk Route, which was a long, long road for traders between China, India and Europe.

AMIR TEMUR

Temur was born in Uzbekistan, in 1336 AD. He was part Mongol and part Turk, and he founded the massive Timurid Empire. When he was a boy, his leg was hurt and he could never walk properly again. This is why some people called him Temur-e-Lang, which means Temur the Lame.

CHENGHIS KHAN

Chenghis Khan was born more than 100 years before Temur, in Mongolia. He was a Mongol, which is where the word Mughal comes from. Chenghis Khan was one of the greatest soldiers and generals ever born, and he founded the Mongol Empire, which became the largest empire in the world. Babur was related to both Temur and Chenghis Khan, as you can see from his Family Tree.

POLO

Polo is a lot like hockey, except you play it on horseback. It was invented hundreds of years ago in the 6th century BC by the Persians.
The Persians took Polo to Central Asia, which is how Babur learned to play it.
The word Polo probably comes from the Tibetan word Pulu, which means Ball.

CHARBAGH

Charbagh means 'Four Gardens'. A Charbagh is a square garden divided into four smaller squares, with walkways for walking and waterways for fountains. The Persians first began making Charbaghs in Persia, and Babur, who loved all kinds of gardens, had them made in Kabul. His favourite Charbagh was the Bagh-e-Wafa.

THE BATTLE OF PANIPAT

Panipat is a small town, about two hours away from Delhi. And the Battle of Panipat is one of the most famous battles in the world. Babur's small army fought Ibrahim Lodi's very big army on the 21st of April 1526, and Babur won. This was the beginning of the Mughal Empire. If you go to Panipat today, you can try and guess where the armies fought, and you can also see where Ibrahim Lodi is buried.

KOHINOOR

Babur and Humayun did not know it then, but the diamond that the king of Gwalior gave Humayun was the famous Kohinoor. The Kohinoor came from the mines of Kollur, in Andhra Pradesh, and it was the biggest diamond in the world. Over many hundred years, it went from king to king, until finally it reached England. And, over many hundred years, people kept cutting it, so it got smaller and smaller. When Nadir Shah saw the diamond, he said it was a Mountain of Light, which is what Koh-i-Noor means in Persian, and that's how it got its name.

GLOSSARY

Anaar	Pomegranate
Bukhari	A heater, in which wood or coal is burned
Chamgidar	Flying bat
Chaqu	Dagger
Dargah	The grave of a Sufi saint
Gilahri	Squirrel
Gul	Rose
Jalghoza	Pinenut
Kamrak	Star fruit
Langur	Monkey with long tail, grey hair and black face
Mahua	The Mahua tree grows in many parts of India. You can eat its flowers, and also make syrup and a special kind of Mahua wine with it
Mirtimuri melons	Babur's favourite melon, which grew only in Fergana
Nashpati	Pear
Nilgai	Blue bull. It is the largest antelope in Asia
Rubab	A musical instrument
Sangtara	Orange
Taup	Cannon

THE BABUR NAMA

The Babur Nama begins like this: "In the month of Ramadan in June 1494, in the province of Fergana, in my twelfth year I became King."

A lot of what we know about Babur, we know because he wrote an autobiography called the Babur Nama. An autobiography is a story you write about your own life, and Babur wrote down almost everything that happened to him after he became King of Fergana. Babur wrote about Umar Shaikh's buttons popping, and he wrote about the Battles of Samarkand and Panipat, and he wrote about all the fruits he ate, the parties he had, and the animals he saw. Babur's sons and grandsons all read his Babur Nama to learn how to be good kings. Babur's grandson Akbar had the book translated into Persian. He also had drawings made, so the book would look special.

WORDS AND LANGUAGES

Babur wrote the Babur Nama in Chaghatai Turkic, which is an old language that nobody speaks any more. He also spoke Persian, which a lot of people still do speak. When people travel, so do words. That's how, when Babur came to India, he and his friends brought along words like *anaar* (pomegranate) and *nashpati* (pear), *chaqu* (dagger) and *taup* (cannon). The *jhalghoza* nuts he found in Kabul are what we call *chilgoza* (pine nuts) in Hindustani today. *Padishah* is how you say King in Persian, and that's how the word *Badshah* came to India. Sometimes, of course, words get a bit stuck. For example, the Persians had never seen coconuts, so they called them *jawz-i-Hind*, which means Indian Walnut. In India, Babur learnt the Hindustani word for them, which is *nariyal*. He learnt many other Hindustani words, too, like *ghari* (time), *kamrak* (star fruit), *gilahri* (squirrel), and *sangtara* (orange). Oranges are also called *narangi* in Hindustani, and *narang* in Sanskrit, and you can see how the word changed as people took oranges with them all over the world:

There was Sanskrit **Narang** and Tamil **Narandam**, Arabic **Naranjah** and Persian **Narenj**, Spanish **Naranja** and Greek **Neratzi**, Italian **Arancia** and English **Orange**. It's a bit like a game of Chinese whisper, isn't it? In fact, the Icelandic word for orange is **Appelsina**, which means Chinese Apple. The Chinese themselves call it **júzi**, which is just completely different from everything else.